CREATIVE WISDOM FOR WRITERS

ROLAND FISHMAN

ALLEN & UNWIN

ROLAND FISHMAN has been a professional writer since 1981. He is an Arts/Law graduate from the University of New South Wales. He spent seven years at *The Sydney Morning Herald*, writing everything from sports columns to features for the *Good Weekend*, and has published two books. He first developed the workshops at The Esalen Institute in California while doing a three month work study program in 1992. He founded The Writers' Studio in 1993 and is currently writing a novel.

The quotes in this book embody the spirit of the courses run by The Writers' Studio. Contact The Writers' Studio at 2/135 Oxford Street, Bondi Junction NSW 2026, telephone (02) 9386 4994, email wstudio@writerstudio.com.au or visit www.writerstudio.com.au

How to use this Book

You can either open it at random
and read a thought for the day,
or you can go through it in order.

It will take you through a process.

We are all creative.

Every day we slaughter our finest impulses. That is why we get a heart-ache when we read those lines written by the hand of a master and recognize them as our own, as the tender shoots which we stifled because we lacked the faith to believe in our own powers, our own criterion of truth and beauty. Every man, when he gets quiet, when he becomes desperately honest with himself, is capable of uttering profound truths. We all derive from the same source. There is no mystery about the origin of things. We are all part of creation, all kings, all poets, all musicians; we have only to open up, only to discover what is already there.

HENRY MILLER

Thinking about writing or
talking about writing or
worrying about writing
is not writing.

It is by sitting down to write every morning that one becomes a writer.

GERALD BRENAN

Don't play small.

Our deepest fear is not that we are inadequate. Our deepest fear is that we are powerful beyond measure. It is our light, not our darkness, that most frightens us. We ask ourselves, who am I to be brilliant, gorgeous, talented and fabulous? Actually, who are you not to be? You are a child of God. Your playing small doesn't serve the world. There's nothing enlightened about shrinking so that other people won't feel insecure around you. We were born to make manifest the glory of God that is within us. It's not just in some of us; it's in everyone. And as we let our own light shine, we unconsciously give other people permission to do the same. As we're liberated from our fear, our presence automatically liberates others.

MARIANNE WILLIAMSON

Commit.

Whatever you can do or dream you can do, begin it.
Boldness has genius, power and magic in it.

JOHANN WOLFGANG VON GOETHE

Writing is a way of life.

I write a little each day without hope and without despair.

ISAK DINESEN

The emotional story is the
most important.

To make you hear, to make you feel . . . to make you *see*. That—and no more, it is everything.

JOSEPH CONRAD

If you want to write, write
and keep writing.

You will get what you want if you work hard and don't die first.

Z<small>EN</small> <small>SAYING</small>

When you are writing a first draft don't worry if what comes out is any good or not. Just write.

If something is worth doing, it is worth doing badly.
JOHN BRADSHAW

You are free to write the worst junk in the universe.
NATALIE GOLDBERG

You will never write a perfect story. Don't even try.

There is a crack in everything God has made.

Ralph Waldo Emerson

The power is in your unconscious.

Most of the work is done in the unconscious.

PETER WEIR

Comedy is about the unconscious. If you can tap into that . . .

ROSEANNE ARNOLD

You cannot control the creative process.

In short we are back to where almost everyone starts: helpless before the process of writing because it obeys inscrutable laws. We are in its power. It is not in ours.

Peter Elbow

Don't judge.

Judgement is part of the writing process. Expect it. Don't let it interfere with the process of writing. Just write.

Syd Field

Tom Wolfe had been a regular journalist when the then editor of *Esquire* magazine, Byron Dobell, asked him to do a story on custom cars. He got horribly blocked. He couldn't seem to write a thing.

So about 8 o'clock that night I started typing the notes out in the form of a memo that began, Dear Byron. I started typing away, starting right with the first time I saw custom cars in California. I just started recording it all, and inside of a couple of hours typing away like a madman, I could tell that something was beginning to happen. By midnight the memo to Byron was 20 pages long and I was still typing like a maniac. I wrapped up the memo about 6.15 am and by this time it was 49 pages long. I took it over to *Esquire* as soon as they opened up, about 9.30 am. About 4 pm I got a call from Byron Dobell. He told me they were striking out the Dear Byron at the top of the memo and running the rest of it in the magazine.

TOM WOLFE

Have fun.

Elmore Leonard, who wrote *Get Shorty*, said he only started getting anywhere when he started having fun.

Have faith.

Like any other art, creative writing is a function of the whole person. The unconscious must flow freely and richly, bringing at demand all the treasures of memory, all the emotions, incidents, scenes, intimations of character and relationship which it has stored away in its depths.

The unconscious is shy, elusive and unwieldy, but it is possible to tap it at will, and even to direct it.

DOROTHEA BRANDE

Don't worry, and don't show off.

. . . do not worry. You have always written before and you will write now. All you have to do is write one true sentence. Write the truest sentence that you know.

ERNEST HEMINGWAY

Don't analyse, just write.

First thoughts are the strongest.

ALLEN GINSBERG

Let the pen do the thinking.

In quickness is truth. The faster you blurt, the more swiftly you write, the more honest you are. In hesitation is thought. In delay comes the effort for a style, instead of leaping upon truth which is the *only* style worth [having].

Ray Bradbury

Writing is an adventure.

On the ridge where the great artist moves forward, every step is an adventure, an extreme risk. In that risk however, and only there, lies the freedom of art. Like all freedom, it is a perpetual risk, an exhausting adventure, and this is why people avoid the risk today, as they avoid liberty with its exacting demands, in order to accept any kind of bondage and achieve at least comfort of soul. But if art is not an adventure, what is it and where is its justification?

ALBERT CAMUS

Don't play safe.

It's a question of what you might do in your wildest imagination, not what you might do because you are bound by the strictures of polite behaviour. We don't want our movies to be bound by that. We'd like our movies to be greatly expressive of our fantasy life.

DAVID MAMET

Caution strangles creativity.

The desire for safety stands against every great and noble enterprise.

TACITUS

God is in the details.

The greatest writers—Homer, Dante, Shakespeare—are effective largely because they deal in particulars and report the details that matter.

WILLIAM STRUNK JNR AND E.B. WHITE

There are three rules to writing
a good story—the trouble is
no one knows what they are.

No rules are universal, including this one.

ANON

Writing is a mood-changing
activity.

I have forced myself to begin writing when I've been utterly exhausted, when I've felt my soul as thin as a playing card, when nothing has seemed worth enduring for another five minutes . . . and somehow the activity of writing changes everything.

JOYCE CAROL OATES

You cannot control the quality
of a first draft, only the quantity.

I write one page of masterpiece to ninety-one pages of shit.

ERNEST HEMINGWAY TO F. SCOTT FITZGERALD

Stay open.

But what if, when you tried to write, you felt stopped, suffocated, and no words came and if they came at all they were wooden and without meaning? What if you had the feeling you could never write another word?

John Hyde Preston

Preston, the way to resume is to resume. It is the only way. So how can you know what it will be? What will be best in it is what you really do not know now. If you knew it all it would not be creation but dictation.

Gertrude Stein

Capture first thoughts.

Don't think.

NATALIE GOLDBERG

The first thought is the strongest.

BOB DYLAN

Just hit the ball.

ALLEN GINSBERG

Your imagination knows the truth and the truth is eternal.

I am certain of nothing but the heart's affections and the truth of the imagination.

JOHN KEATS

Writing and editing are separate tasks. Mix them at your peril.

The habit of compulsive, premature editing doesn't just make writing hard. It also makes writing dead.

PETER ELBOW

Write to a schedule.

Angels only began shining when they achieved discipline.
Rumi

The power is in the story.

For writers who can tell a quality story it is a seller's market. Always has been, always will.

ROBERT MCKEE

You can't sprint in a marathon.

Remember to stop while you are still going good. That keeps it moving instead of having it die whenever you go on and write yourself out. When you do that you find that the next day you are pooped and can't go on.

ERNEST HEMINGWAY

Write for the fun of it.

It was really more fun than anything. That was really why you did it. He had never realised that before. It wasn't conscious. It was simply that it was the greatest pleasure. It had more bite to it than anything else.

Ernest Hemingway

Have a go.

Jump. It is not as wide as you think.

JOSEPH CAMPBELL

Writing is a craft.

Anxious, inexperienced writers obey rules; rebellious, unschooled writers break the rules; an artist masters the form.

Robert McKee

When writing, don't listen to
your inner critic.

I've told every young writer I know to do the job all the way through even if they think it is no good . . . All writers are discontented with their work as it's being made. That's because they are always aware of a potential, and believe they're not reaching it. But the reader is not aware of the potential so it makes no difference to him.

WILLIAM SAROYAN

You'll never be perfect.

Lower your standards and keep going.
WILLIAM STAFFORD

Work on one thing at a time.

Put all your eggs in one basket, and then watch that basket.

Andrew Carnegie

When you write, don't think
about the outcome.

You have the right to work, but for the work's sake only. You have no right to the fruits of work. Desire for the fruits of work must never be your motive in working. Never give way to laziness either. Work done with anxiety about results is far inferior to work done without such anxiety. They who work selfishly for results are miserable.

THE BHAGAVAD-GITA

The perfect is the enemy of the good.

What I have done all through my work is to repeat: 'This is the best I can do; take it or leave it.' Or again: 'If it isn't literature, call it what you like. I don't give a damn.'

HENRY MILLER

You can't judge your own work.

It is . . . important to remember that all writers are notoriously inconstant in their attitudes toward their work; the value they accord any given work will shift and change from moment to moment like the weather. A 'final' judgement is virtually impossible to reach and for many reasons this is a good thing.

Victoria Nelson

Just do it.

People ask: What if I unblock myself and I have nothing to say? The more pertinent question is what if I live my life without giving myself the opportunity to express what I need to say?

JULIA CAMERON

Writers need goals.

The fact that pearls exist makes divers glad.

RUMI

Success comes from high hopes combined with daily discipline.

ZIG ZIGGLER

Go for the emotion.

Only emotion endures.

EZRA POUND

Let your pen do the thinking.

How do I know what I think until I see what I say?

E.M. FORSTER

Stay in the moment.

Why can't I be as great as Tolstoy, *now*? Well, a voice whispers from within, *maybe I am*. Maybe this very sentence I am in the act of composing will someday be memorized by schoolchildren and—

Victoria Nelson

Put yourself on the line.

By not writing, one is obeying the urgent inner command not to define oneself, not to grow and develop into that sad and limited creature, minor (or possibly even a never-published) poet or whatever. Instead one stays interesting, *potentially* great the rest of one's life.

Victoria Nelson

It's how you say it.

A writer has to master his craft and learn the rules before he tries to break them. It's much more than just feeling that you have something to say. You have to learn how to say it.

Arthur Kopit

Judgement kills creativity.

Make this a rule: always remember that your Censor's negative opinions are not the truth. This takes practice.

JULIA CAMERON

Persistence outstrips all
other virtues.

Anyone can become a writer, the trick is staying a writer.

HARLAN ELLISON

The mastery of any art is the work of a lifetime.

EZRA POUND

The theory is simple, but by no means easy.

Like all novice writers his understanding of the theory lagged behind his ability to put it into practice.

MICHAEL REYNOLDS ON ERNEST HEMINGWAY

Writing is a way of life.

We are all apprentices in a craft where no one ever becomes a master.

ERNEST HEMINGWAY

Experiment.

Finding the right form for your story is simply to realize the most *natural* way of telling the story.

TRUMAN CAPOTE

Writing fiction challenges you.

Writing is like a contact sport, like football. Why do kids play football? They can get hurt on any play, can't they? Yet they can't wait until Saturday comes around. Writing is like that. You can get hurt, but you enjoy it.

IRWIN SHAW

Nobody knows anything.

Dear Herr Doctor:

You are already ten months behind with the manuscript of *Das Kapital*, which you have agreed to write for us. If we do not receive the manuscript within six months, we shall be obliged to commission another to do this work.

LETTER TO KARL MARX FROM HIS LEIPZIG PUBLISHER

Don't be afraid of the squiggly path.

Improvement makes strait roads; but the crooked roads without Improvement are roads of Genius.

WILLIAM BLAKE

Writing nourishes the spirit.

We . . . write to heighten our own awareness of life . . .
We write to taste life twice, in the moment and in retro-
spection . . . We write to be able to transcend our life,
to reach beyond it . . . to teach ourselves to speak with
others.

ANAÏS NIN

Let your writing find its own course.

What's important to remember is that you're just fooling around. What you're doing isn't serious. It 'doesn't count'. It's play. In the beginning, before it was duty, art was child's play.

VICTORIA NELSON

We are our own worst enemies.

The opponent in this game is inside us. It is that part of our psychological make-up that creates imagined limitations, passes destructive judgements, and whittles away at our self confidence—sometimes with an axe.

Barry Green

The important thing is to keep going.

You must once and for all give up being worried about successes and failures. Don't let that concern you. It's your duty to go on working steadily day by day, quite steadily, to be prepared for mistakes, which are inevitable, and for failures.

ANTON CHEKHOV

Kill the internal editor.

Nothing is so distracting, during the heat of creation, as the carping, niggling, nitpicking voice of critical judgement.

VICTORIA NELSON

Be generous.

Your depression is connected to your insolence and refusal to praise. Whoever feels himself walking on the path, and refuses to praise—that man or woman steals from others every day—is a shoplifter.

RUMI

Don't take it personally.

We have read your manuscript with boundless delight. If we were to publish your paper, it would be impossible for us to publish any work of lower standard. And as it is unthinkable that in the next thousand years we shall see its equal, we are, to our regret, etc.

REJECTION SLIP FROM A CHINESE ECONOMICS JOURNAL, QUOTED IN THE *FINANCIAL TIMES*

You need a process.

The conscious mind is going to suggest the obvious, the cliché, because these things offer the security of having succeeded in the past. Only the mind that has been taken off itself and put on a task is allowed true creativity.

DAVID MAMET

Get through the first draft as
quickly as possible.

Begin at the beginning, go through to the end, *then* stop.

LEWIS CARROLL

Keep going.

It does not matter how slowly you go, so long as you do not stop.

Confucius

Don't be attached to what
comes out of your pen.

The Great Way is not difficult for those who have no preferences.

SENGSTAN, THIRD ZEN PATRIARCH

We write to rewrite.

Tolstoy went through and rewrote *War and Peace* eight times and was still making corrections in the galleys. Things like this should hearten every writer whose first drafts are dreadful, like mine are.

RAYMOND CARVER

Write about whom you wish
to become.

What does the writer want out of life? What does he want to become? These are the things he should write about. The question is who do I wish to become?

COLIN WILSON

Feel the fear and do it.

Nothing kills the will to work more surely than contemplating the entirety of the work when all we need do is engage the work right before our eyes.

Eric Maisel

Write one story at a time.

Work on one thing at a time until finished. Start no more new books . . . Forget the books you want to write. Think only of the book you *are* writing.

HENRY MILLER

Have a program.

Work according to program, not according to mood. Stop at the appointed time . . . Discard the program when you feel like it—but go back to it the next day.

HENRY MILLER

Don't take yourself and your writing too seriously.

Don't be nervous. Work calmly, joyously, recklessly on whatever is at hand . . . Don't be a draught-horse! Work with pleasure only.

Henry Miller

Make writing a priority.

Write first and always. Painting, music, friends, cinema, all these come afterwards.

Henry Miller

Dream.

We read a few words at the beginning of the book or the particular story, and suddenly we find ourselves seeing not words on a page but a train moving through Russia, an old Italian crying, or a farmhouse battered by rain.

JOHN GARDNER

Be bold.

The bold imagination produces great art; the timid one small art.

NORTHROP FRYE

Push yourself.

The characters in my novels are my own unrealized possibilities . . . Each one has crossed a border I myself have circumvented . . . beyond that border begins the secret the novel asks about . . .

MILAN KUNDERA

Let go of your plan.

The samurai goes into battle with a plan. But when the fighting starts he is in the moment.

The archer has a target, but he doesn't take aim.

ZEN SAYINGS

Create moral dilemmas.

In the final analysis, real suspense comes with moral dilemma and the courage to make and act upon choices. False suspense comes from the accidental and meaningless occurrence of one dammed thing after another.

JOHN GARDNER

Don't work obsessively.

Often when one works at a hard question, nothing good is accomplished at the first attack. Then one takes a rest, longer or shorter, and sits down anew to the work. During the first half-hour, as before, nothing is found, and then all of a sudden the decisive idea presents itself to the mind.

HENRI POINCARÉ

Take one step at a time.

I used to work in bursts of intuition. Now I find the very process of working step by step feeds my imagination.

ANNE TRUITT

Stories evolve.

I know that my original idea for a story is going to be only the point of departure for something that will push me in an unexpected way.

MARIO VARGAS LLOSA

It doesn't matter if none of your first draft is any good.

The first draft of a book is the most uncertain—where you need guts, the ability to accept the imperfect until it is better.

Bernard Malamud

Take chances.

If you can't be a genius, imitate the daring.

EUDORA WELTY

Discover your story in
the writing.

It is essential to remember that the creative end is never in full sight at the beginning and that it is brought wholly into view only when the process of creation is completed.

BREWSTER GHEISLIN

Less is more.

Not that the story need be long, but it takes a long while to make it short.

HENRY DAVID THOREAU

Writing a story is a process.

I very much believe in the principle of superabundance and the attendant principle of cutting back. You can always take out or change, but you cannot always put in.

JAMES DICKEY

Write your story.

It's never too late to be who you might have been.

GEORGE ELIOT

Stories move towards
completion.

Pictures moved toward their completion by progression. Each day brought something new. A picture was a sum of additions. With me, a picture is a sum of destructions. I make a picture, and proceed to destroy it. But in the end nothing is lost; the red I have removed from one part shows up in another.

PABLO PICASSO

Find the essence.

If you can't put it into a sentence you haven't got a story.

BRYCE COURTNEY

First drafts are a time of uncertainty.

Writing a first draft is like groping one's way into a dark room, or overhearing a faint conversation, or telling a joke whose punch line you've forgotten. As someone said, one writes mainly to rewrite, for rewriting and revising are how one's mind comes to inhabit the material fully.

TED SOLOTAROFF

Detach.

The trouble is that when you're just beginning to write, you may believe that words committed to paper are sacred, fixed, immutable. But you're not dealing with a finished, printed, copyrighted book, only with an idea, a pile of words that change shape many times before they take shape as a book.

DOROTHY BRYANT

First drafts should be messy.

The first attempts are absolutely unbearable. I say this because I want you to know that if you see something worth while in what I am doing, it is not by accident but because of real intention and purpose.

VINCENT VAN GOGH

Try things.

Write several short openings to the same story . . .
Don't consciously judge these openings. Instead, keep
producing variations . . . Once you've done this a few
times, you'll become quite adept at producing these by
merely methodically moving through the possibilities.
And, inevitably, one of the variations will click in your
mind, and you'll feel a sense of rightness and eagerness—
'Yes this is it.' That is one of the major pleasures in
writing fiction.

Nancy Kress

Don't revise it. Rewrite it.

What I tend to do is not so much pick at a thing but sit down and rewrite it completely. After making notes on one draft I'd sit down and rewrite it again from the beginning. I've found that's much better than patching and amputating things. One has to rethink the thing completely. They say D.H. Lawrence used to write second drafts and never look at the first.

Christopher Isherwood

Don't be consumed by ambition.

On becoming too ambitious we then expect that our efforts should generate visible progress. We must be willing to see things through without looking for visible progress. Only a steady, persevering disengagement and inner independence, by which we remain true to our higher nature, will win in the end.

I CHING

Have a goal and let it go.

Danger comes from wanting, from fearing, and from being ambitiously goal-oriented instead of perseveringly path-oriented. We abandon the slow, step-by-step work that creates enduring change.

I Ching

Sit with the tension.

Danger also refers to an inner pressure to do something simply to end the ambiguity of the situation.

I CHING

Don't explain.

The guy says to the girl, 'that's a lovely dress'—he does not say, 'I haven't been laid in six weeks.'

DAVID MAMET

Write a number of drafts.

Here's how you write a play. You do a lot of writing to figure out what the hell the play's about and throw away three-quarters of that and write it again and find out what that play's about and throw out three-quarters of it and write it again.

DAVID MAMET

Imagine.

Imagination is more important than knowledge.

ALBERT EINSTEIN

Creativity requires work.

The artistic impulse seems not to wish to produce finished work. It certainly deserts us halfway, after the idea is born; and if we go on, art is labor.

CLARENCE DAY

Let go.

All that can be done is take the existing material and discard nine-tenths of it.

FRANK RINES

Words on paper are not sacred.

To rewrite ten times is not unusual.

SAUL BELLOW

Fewer words often say more.

Concentrate. Narrow down. Exclude.

HENRY MILLER

Keep it simple.

If I started to write elaborately, or like someone intro-
ducing or presenting something, I found that I could cut
that scrollwork or ornament out and throw it away and
start with the first true simple declarative sentence I had
written.

Ernest Hemingway

Serve the reader.

When talented people write well, it is generally for this reason: they're moved by a desire to touch the audience.

Robert McKee

Make every word count.

A sentence should contain no unnecessary words, a paragraph no unnecessary sentences, for the same reason that a drawing should have no unnecessary lines and a machine no unnecessary parts. This requires not that a writer should make all sentences short or avoid all detail . . . but that every word tell.

WILLIAM STRUNK JNR AND E.B. WHITE

Kill your darlings.

Read over your compositions, and where ever you meet with a passage you think is particularly fine, strike it out.

SAMUEL JOHNSON

Focus on the effect of the whole.

Everything Max does is directed toward the whole effect of the book . . . He can take a mess of chaos, give you the scaffold, and then you build a house on it.

MARCIA DAVENPORT ON MAX PERKINS' EDITING

Work hard.

Genius is the infinite capacity for taking pains.

ALBERT EINSTEIN

When you take out what is not meant to be in your story, it becomes clear what should be in your story.

The really incredible thing was that once the extraneous matter was removed, once the unfinished fragments and great chunks of stuff that did not belong in the books were taken out, the parts that remained fell into place and fitted together like the pieces of a jigsaw puzzle.

EDWARD ASWELL ON MAX PERKINS' EDITING

You need plenty of raw material.

All I do is carve away everything that isn't the sculpture.

MICHELANGELO

Editing can hurt.

To revise, all you have to do is take away everything that isn't the story. It's especially tough to take out a scene that may be very good, but bad for the story as a whole.

DAVID KAPLAN

Only describe what is important
to the story.

You don't need to describe the kitchen, only where the carving knife is.

BRYCE COURTNEY

Editing makes all the difference.

The difference between me and an amateur is I cut out the boring bits.

ELMORE LEONARD

Your unconscious has the
answers.

If you put a poem aside, when you look at it again it tends to rewrite itself.

STEPHEN SPENDER

Keep going.

I see the notion of talent as quite irrelevant. I see instead old-fashioned notions of perseverance, application, industry . . . It comes down in every instance to this dualism between what one wants and what one may be afraid to have.

GORDON LISH

Talent equals work.

If the power to do hard work is not talent, it is the best substitute for it.

JAMES A. GARFIELD

Be wild.

Everyone has talent. What is rare is the courage to follow that talent to the dark place where it leads.

Erica Jong

Don't show off.

No tricks.

RAYMOND CARVER

Don't abandon your story.

One worthwhile task carried to a successful conclusion is worth half a hundred half-finished tasks.

B.C. FORBES

Challenge yourself.

Write about something that will change your life. It is the best gift you can give yourself.

JOHN TRUBY

Get to the end and stop.

There is only one thing to do with a novel and that is to go straight on through to the end of the damn thing.

Ernest Hemingway to F. Scott Fitzgerald

There's no feeling like
having written.

It's hard to get to the finish of your story and feel that special sense of satisfaction of Having Written unless you plow through to the end as directly and quickly as you can.

DAVID KAPLAN

It ain't over until it is over.

. . . endings, man, they weren't as easy as they looked.

CHILI PALMER IN ELMORE LEONARD'S *GET SHORTY*

First published in 2000

Allen & Unwin
9 Atchison Street
St Leonards NSW 2065
Australia
Phone: (61 2) 8425 0100
Fax: (61 2) 9906 2218
Email: frontdesk@allen-unwin.com.au
Web: http://www.allen-unwin.com.au

National Library of Australia
Cataloguing-in-Publication entry:

Fishman, Roland, 1955– .
Creative wisdom for writers.

ISBN 1 86508 336 4.

1. Authorship—Quotations, maxims, etc.
2. Encouragement. I. Title.

808.02

Book design by Phil Campbell
Set in Perpetua by DOCUPRO, Sydney
Printed by Australian Print Group,
Maryborough, Vic.

10 8 6 4 2 1 3 5 7 9